Original title:
A Houseplant's Wish

Copyright © 2025 Creative Arts Management OÜ
All rights reserved.

Author: Franklin Stone
ISBN HARDBACK: 978-1-80581-905-9
ISBN PAPERBACK: 978-1-80581-432-0
ISBN EBOOK: 978-1-80581-905-9

Wishes Growing in the Dark

In shadows deep, I plot my dreams,
A leaf of green with silly schemes.
I long for sun, a bright parade,
To dance and twirl, not just cascade.

Please pass the light, I'm feeling blue,
A lamp will do, not quite a zoo.
With whispered hopes on petals wide,
I wish for friends, not just the tide.

The Language of Leafy Letters

In every leaf, I whisper tales,
My roots are snickering, with no fails.
I dream of soil, rich and warm,
To write my notes, let laughter swarm.

I'd send a message through a breeze,
A shout-out to my garden trees.
In every rustle, secrets spin,
A leafy language, let's begin!

Hues of Hope Against the Wall

Against the wall, I paint my dreams,
In polka dots of varied schemes.
Oh how I wish for rainbow friends,
To spread my joy as daylight blends.

A splash of purple, a dash of red,
I giggle as colors fill my head.
What fun it is to grow so bright,
In hues of hope, from day to night!

The Comfort of Companionship

Oh, here we sit, the pots all snug,
A leafy crew, we laugh and hug.
With every droplet, we share a chat,
My dearest pals, we're quite the brat!

In whispers soft, we root for fun,
Through storms and breezes, we all run.
Companions in this sunny space,
Together let's find our happy place.

An Odyssey in Green

In the corner, I stand so bright,
Every day I stretch for light.
With leaf and stem, I do my best,
Hoping for some photosynthesized rest.

Oh, if only I had feet to roam,
I'd dance around this little home.
I'd tiptoe past the sleeping cat,
And find a spot that's nice and fat.

Lost Among the Shadows

Hiding here from duster's might,
Shadows play in the pale moonlight.
Dust bunnies make a cozy bed,
But I'd rather snuggle in my spread.

A little sunlight, a bit of care,
But all I get is the chilly air.
I wish on stars for a sunny break,
And maybe someone to give me a shake!

The Yearn for Growth

Each morning, I reach for the sky,
With dreams of being oh so spry.
A sprout today, a tree at night,
Why can't they see my true delight?

They water me with love and glee,
Yet here I am, just wee ol' me.
Imagine the day I'd break the pot,
And dance around like I own the lot!

Tending to the Soul

Oh, please don't let me wilt away,
With quirky words, I plead and sway.
A little water, a chat, a tune,
I'll bloom like crazy if you follow soon!

Let's face the facts, it's a funny game,
I want to grow, but not alone in fame.
So grab a pot and let's begin,
Together we'll laugh and let the fun spin!

Reflections in the Glass

In the window I peek, not a soul in sight,
Just a dust bunny floating, oh what a fright!
Dirt on my leaves, I demand a sweep,
Come on, human, I need my beauty sleep!

I watch the world pass, they're all so free,
While I stay put, sipping water, you see.
The neighbor's cat laughs at my plight,
Oh for a garden party, just one night!

Craving the Open Air

Oh, how I long for a breeze on my face,
To stretch out my tendrils in a wide open space.
Instead, I'm stuck here on this dusty shelf,
Just a plain green buddy, no wildness for self.

If I could just dance in the sun for a while,
You'd see my petals bloom, maybe even smile.
But here I will sit, just soaking in light,
Wishing for freedom while you nap at night.

Tendrils of Desire

My little tendrils twist and they flow,
Reaching for something, but where do they go?
They tickle the curtain, entangle the chair,
Oh, how I dream of living with flair!

Just once I'd like to escape out the door,
To wrap 'round a tree or swing by the shore.
But alas, I'm stuck, in this pot, oh so cozy,
Dreaming of forests, a life just so rosy!

Leaves That Dream

My leaves whisper secrets, oh what a blast,
Of running through gardens, having a vast…
Adventure in soil, so rich and divine,
Peeking at butterflies, sipping sweet wine!

With each little flutter, my hopes start to soar,
Perhaps I'll break free, just open that door.
But until that day comes, I'll laugh in my pot,
Sipping on sunshine, it's all that I've got!

The Unseen Threads of Time

In the corner I stand, small and bright,
Wondering home is such a delight,
Photosynthesis all day is just cool,
But I dream of my own swimming pool!

Sunshine beams down, I dance and sway,
But why can't I travel far away?
I've seen the new cat strut outside,
But I'm stuck here, nowhere to hide!

Just a little dirt, please let me roam,
Finding some soil to call my own,
But here I stay, in this pot so tight,
Plotting my escape by the moonlight!

Oh, the stories I'd tell if I could speak,
Of the dog who barks and the ants that sneak,
Maybe one day, I'll sprout little feet,
And together we'll dance to a groovy beat!

Flourishing in the Shadows

In the shadows, I do my best,
With sunlight barely, I take a rest,
Lurking in corners, I hear the chat,
Of humans, I wish I could be part of that!

Just a leaf, but oh what a plan,
To sway in the breeze like a confident man,
When the sun beams down, I'll strut my stuff,
With a cheeky grin saying, 'Isn't this tough?'

Pats on the head, flowers in pots,
Everyone else gets all the hot shots,
But when it rains, I have my fun,
Dancing droplets? Oh, I'm number one!

So here's to the shade, let's toast with glee,
Even if I'm stuck, I'm wild and free,
With each little sprout, I find my way,
Flourishing boldly, come what may!

Vows of Verdant Hope

A tiny green sprout with dreams so grand,
Choosing my pot, the best in the land,
I whisper to petals, soft and sweet,
'Wait until spring, then we'll take to the street!'

I see the birds fly above me high,
While I'm here rooted, oh me, oh my!
But when the wind blows, I wobble and cheer,
Planning for moments when the coast is clear!

With friends all around, the thorns and blooms,
We vow to break out of these dusty rooms,
Let's go on adventures, we'll float and glide,
Together we'll roll, with nature as our guide!

So here's to us, the green brigade,
Making promises in sunshine so staid,
For every leaf's dream, there's a hope so pure,
One day we'll flourish, of that I'm sure!

Beneath the Windowpane's Gaze

In sunlight's hug, oh how I thrive,
I'm a leafy star, oh so alive.
Ignoring the dust, I stretch and sway,
Hoping for pizza crumbs every day.

The cat thinks I'm a jungle beast,
As she eyes my leaves, it's quite the feast.
I giggle as she leaps with grace,
But I'm just here, my leafy space.

If only I could dance and sing,
Wishing for a day that I could bring.
A pot of joy and fun to share,
With every window's sunny glare.

So here I stand, with roots so deep,
Counting my dreams, oh, what a leap!
Perhaps a friend, a cactus tall,
To join me in this sunlit hall.

The Song of Soil and Water

Listen closely, I sing a tune,
A melody by the light of the moon.
With drops of water, I sway and hum,
Dreaming of flavor, like tasty gum.

Oh soil, rich bed, my cozy throne,
With each little worm, I feel so grown.
We dance in pots, three steps, then sway,
Every leaf a note in this garden ballet.

When the sun peeks, I raise my head,
Wishing for chocolate, instead of bread.
If only I could munch on some goo,
Like syrupy nectar or sweet fondue!

So here's to life, a silly spree,
With every drip, I giggle with glee.
In my leafy kingdom, I'll sway and sway,
Singing my song, come what may.

A Heartbeat in a Fern

The fronds unfold, a secret dance,
Each day a chance for leafy romance.
I quiver and shake with the slightest breeze,
Wishing for handfuls of tasty cheese.

Tiny bugs, a feast to behold,
Oh, to munch visions of riches untold!
With surprise attacks from a curious cat,
It's a battle of hearts, and I'm loving that.

If only my leaves could chat back,
I'd spill my dreams, a silly knack.
I'd tell of dandelions in wide-open fields,
And the jellybeans that sunlight yields.

Yet here I thrive, in this snug pot,
Daydreaming antics, quite a lot.
So I'll wiggle and jive, through thick and thin,
In my ferny world, I always win!

Secrets of the Indoor Jungle

In the corner, I've made my stand,
With dusty leaves, I rule this land.
Please don't mind my awkward pose,
I'm just waiting for the door to close.

The lights above flicker and blink,
Here in the jungle, I simply think.
Wouldn't it be grand to grow up tall,
And occasionally stand, proud and all?

I overheard a giggle from the broom,
It whispered tales of more leafy room.
If only I could stretch my arms wide,
And let my dreams, oh my goodness, glide!

So here we squat, in pots so tight,
Living the life in this half-lit sight.
Let's share a laugh as we sit and sip,
On dreams of sun-kissed jungle trips!

A Leaf's Surrender

I long to stretch beyond this pot,
But jokes on me, I'm stuck a lot.
The sun outside, it looks so bright,
Yet here I sit, oh what a plight.

My friends, the weeds, they laugh out loud,
With freedom found, they feel so proud.
I wiggle leaves and play a game,
Yet still I yield, how quite the shame.

I'll plot and scheme from this green space,
To sneak a peak at life's great race.
With every inch, I plot my coup,
Oh, what a sight I'd be to you!

But here I am, just taking root,
While ants parade in their cute suit.
A daily dose of water's nice,
Yet dreams of running are my vice.

Wishes Wrapped in Chlorophyll

Oh, to be a butterfly so free,
Fluttering around, what glee that'd be!
Instead, I'm here, just sipping light,
Wishing for wings, oh what a sight!

I mime the dance of graceful blooms,
While shaking off the dusty glooms.
With every breeze, I sway and sway,
But inwardly, I yearn to play!

I hear the flowers gossip near,
About grand adventures far and dear.
While I, in silence, watch their tale,
Their bold escapes make my heart pale.

Yet still I sing my verdant song,
In clumsy hums, I carry on.
For dreams are wrapped in leaves like me,
And someday, maybe I'll break free!

The Breath of a Potted Dream

In this little pot, I dream of flight,
With my roots firm, I'm stuck here tight.
But oh, what visions I hold dear,
Of wandering far, without a fear.

If I could stretch above the wall,
I'd dance and twist, I'd have a ball!
The sunlit rays would cheer me on,
As I twirled 'round until I'm gone.

But here I sip on morning dew,
With spider webs as my view.
I plot my moves each passing day,
While neighbors stare, what can I say?

Yet in this spot, I sow my cheer,
With every breeze, I'll persevere.
Oh, dreams take root and branches grow,
In this little pot, I'll steal the show!

Thoughtful Tendrils

With tendrils twisty, I reach and stretch,
But oh, this planter's quite the sketch!
I dream of climbing a grand tall tree,
Instead, I hug this pot, it's just me.

To inch and crawl, I plot my scheme,
While watching ants, I dare to dream.
With every leaf, I craft my plan,
To worm my way to freedom's span.

The sunbeam's warmth, my only flair,
Yet here I sit, a potted chair.
I whisper secrets to the soil,
Of grand adventures that I foil.

So if you wonder what I'm worth,
Just know that dreams are here on Earth.
With every twist and every turn,
A little humor is what I yearn!

Whispers from the Roots

In the pot, I dream awake,
Wishing I could stretch and shake.
A sunny dance, a leafy prance,
Just a little chance to enhance.

With every drip of water's fall,
I hope to grow, to stand up tall.
But here I sit, just sipping light,
Plotting schemes to reach the height.

A friendly spider passes by,
I whisper secrets to the sky.
"I crave the breeze, a trip outdoors,
Help me escape these tiny pores!"

What's a plant without a little fun?
I'm craving sun! Oh, just one run!
Through the room, I'll wiggle and sway,
One day I'll sprout wings and fly away!

The Secret of the Soil

In dirt so rich, I plot and scheme,
What's buried deep? Oh, I can dream!
Worms are my friends, they chat a lot,
Gossiping 'bout their cozy spot.

"I'd wear a hat if I had a head,
To block the sun when I'm in bed!
But here I grow, all leafy green,
In a pot that's fit for a queen!"

Sometimes I wish for feet to roam,
To break free from this indoor home.
A little soil, a tiny root,
Let's gather friends and start a flute!

With every drop of rain that falls,
I throw a party, and it calls!
The fungi dance, the snails groove slow,
In the secret soil, let's put on a show!

Beneath the Window's Embrace

Sunbeams splash upon my face,
Beneath this window, such a space!
I tap dance on my leafy toes,
Dreaming of adventures where nobody knows.

"Knock, knock," says a bug with flair,
"Mind if I rest? It's sunny air!"
I say, "Join in, let's share a laugh,
While we sunbathe and sip the half!"

The curtains sway like a party flag,
I ask the breeze for just one brag.
"Oh, tell the world I'm the best green!
Look at my leaves, so bright and keen!"

In this patch of warmth, we celebrate,
With a wink and nod, we cultivate.
A jolly gang of vibrant cheer,
Beneath this window, nothing's drear!

Rain's Gentle Caress

Oh, how I love a rainy day,
It's like a spa, I must say!
Each droplet's kiss, a nimble dance,
In my leafy home, I take a chance.

The clouds roll in; I stretch with glee,
A little rain, oh, let it be!
The pitter-patter, oh so sweet,
Makes my roots wiggle with a beat.

The neighbors glance, they laugh and stare,
"A dancing plant? That's quite rare!"
But I just smile, soaking through,
In this green world, we'll start anew!

So here I sway, the rain my friend,
With every drop, the fun won't end.
I'll sprout a dream, a joyful ploy,
In each sweet puddle, I find my joy!

Echoes of a Forgotten Garden

In a pot with love I dwell,
Waiting for some tales to tell.
A sip of sun, a splash of rain,
Yet I pine for a bit of fame.

What if I could strut and pose?
Become the star of all plant shows!
Dance in light with leaves held high,
Tease the shadows passing by.

Oh, to be a fern so wild,
Swinging free, a daring child.
Instead, I sit, quite misunderstood,
Dreaming big in my little wood.

So here I am, quite rooted still,
With visions of a plant-filled thrill.
If only I could break the mold,
And bask in stories yet untold.

Serenity in Stems

Petal by petal, I scheme and plot,
Yearning for the life, the wild, the hot.
To twirl in breezes, dance in light,
Instead, I sip on dust each night.

Oh, to wiggle in the corner bright,
To be the envy in daylight's sight.
Yet here I wait, still in my chair,
Practicing my poses, with ample care.

Each tiny leaf a secret wish,
For a nibble of cake, or a juicy dish.
But here I sit, a loyal chap,
Dreaming of life beyond my pap.

Perhaps one day I'll snag a vine,
Claim all the sun, make it mine.
Till then, I'll sway with all my might,
Hoping to sprout in the moonlight.

Potted Aspirations

In my pot, I dream of glee,
Of exploring places, wild and free.
But here I squish, in dirt, confined,
A potted prince, oh how unrefined!

If I could leap like dandelions bold,
Make friends with bees, feel the sun's gold.
Instead, I play the waiting game,
Staring at the window, feeling lame.

To drink a soda, taste sweet pie,
Or take a stroll 'neath the blue sky.
Yet here I'll grow, through thick and thin,
Grasping dreams of where I've been.

So here's to sprouts and roots below,
To whispered hopes, and the love that grows.
Though I may stay, I laugh and grin,
For one day, surely, I'll break out and win!

Green Fingers of Fate

With fingers green and dreams of gold,
I watch my leaves, and feel quite bold.
To twist, to turn, to spring and sway,
Instead, I stand, and count the day.

In corners high, where light is shy,
I wish to dance, to reach the sky.
Yet here I sit on this old shelf,
Dreaming hard of another self.

A cactus might just steal the show,
While I stay humble, lying low.
I'll sprinkle joy, I'll eavesdrop in,
And plot my escape with a cheeky grin.

So raise a glass to leaves a-turn,
For every plant has hope to burn.
With each new sprout, I'll sing my tune,
Of green ambitions, under the moon.

Embracing the Rays

Oh, sunbeam, where are you hiding?
I swear I saw you gliding.
My leaves are thirsty, please come near,
Without your warmth, I fear, I fear!

Window sills, my favorite spot,
Dreaming of a bright sun plot.
Just a little touch of light,
Make my green heart feel so right!

I twist and turn to catch that glow,
Like a plant diva, stealing the show.
Solar power, it's my delight,
Not too heavy, just a slight bite!

When clouds roll in, I start to sulk,
Without my rays, I feel like bulk.
Come back soon, my starry friend,
So I can dance, and not pretend!

Whispers of Greenery

A lilting breeze, how sweet you are,
I dream of travel and flying far.
But stuck in this pot, so snug and tight,
Can I ride the wind? Oh, what a sight!

My leaves are fluttering in delight,
While birds above take off in flight.
"Adventure calls!" I want to shout,
But who would take this pot about?

I long to sway with giants tall,
Not just listen to the raindrops fall.
Oh, to see the world beyond,
Instead of just this little pond!

In the corner, I sing to the wall,
Imagining I'm daring and tall.
But what good is a dream so grand,
When my roots are stuck in this bland land?

Longing in Sunlight

A patch of sun, I grinch and pout,
Why can't I move, is it a drought?
Each photon feels like pure delight,
Yet here I sit, out of the light!

My neighbors bask and soak it up,
While I just wait, a plastic cup.
"Give me warmth!" I plea in vain,
Without that glow, it's all mundane.

I stretch my leaves, I wiggle and wail,
In quest of rays, I will prevail.
A sunbeam's hug is my only goal,
Let it flow, enrich my soul!

So come, dear sun, don't be so shy,
Turn your face and let me fly.
For every hour without your shine,
Is a sad plant's tale, oh so divine!

Dreams of Sheltered Roots

Digging down in my cozy earth,
Counting blessings and my worth.
Yet sometimes I peek up in glee,
What lies beyond this pot for me?

With roots so snug, I giggle and play,
Though deep inside, I wish for sway.
Could I stroll past the window's glare?
Finding adventures, oh, to dare!

The soil feels nice, but let's be real,
A garden party would be a steal.
To mingle with friends, lush and bold,
And share the tales nobody told!

So bring on the light, and invite some fun,
Let's dance together, one by one.
In dreams of roots so bold and free,
Just a little more space for me!

The Breath of Indoor Life

In a pot on the sill, I dream of the sun,
With leaves stretching wide, oh, this could be fun!
But who is that creature, with fur and with paws?
My friend, the cat-thief, with no planty laws.

Water me, please, I beg with my sprout,
But you forget, and I start to pout.
I'd shake my roots, if I could, you see,
To remind you of me, your leafy decree!

A dance in the breeze, oh, what a delight,
To sway and to shimmy in the warm, soft light.
Yet here I am stuck, in my little green space,
While you prance around—what a life I must chase!

So here's to my dreams of the garden outside,
Where sunflowers stand tall, and the daisies abide.
I'll keep on growing, despite all my strife,
Waiting for days that bring me to life.

Petals of Hope and Harmony

Oh, how I long for the rain's gentle kiss,
To wash off the dust, what a glorious bliss!
But then there's the vacuum, oh what a fright,
Zipping 'round corners, stealing my light.

Each time you forget, I'm drooping with woe,
Wishing for friends in the window to grow.
An awkward old fern, a cactus with flair,
But here I sit lonely, gasping for air.

If you think I'm quiet, it's just my facade,
For I dream of adventures that seem quite bizarre.
To tango with ferns or to join in the fun,
With petals and pollen, we'd party 'til done.

So, little human, pour extra, who cares?
Let's water the gossip, share secrets in pairs.
For every leaf whispers a tale or a quip,
In this little green world, let laughter equip.

Journeying through the Seasons

In spring, I sprout with a delicate cheer,
Waving my leaves, call the sun to come near.
But summer arrives, I'm cooking in heat,
With dreams of a breeze and some feet on the street.

Then autumn comes dancing, oh what a sight!
Colors of gold, but not too much light.
I'm stuck in my pot while the world spins away,
Resigned to my fate, oh, what a cliché!

But winter's a blizzard, all white and so cold,
With frost on my petals, I'm feeling quite bold.
I toss a few jokes to the dust bunnies near,
Who chuckle and scoff, but they still disappear.

So here's to the gardens both wild and unseen,
Where critters abound and the air feels so clean.
In every strange season, I dream and I sway,
For every petal's wish is a story to play.

Aspirations in Chlorophyll

With a thirst for some adventure, I quietly sigh,
If only my pot was a little more high!
To see all the world from a leafy high view,
I'd wear a small crown, just call me your rue.

I appreciate sunshine, and I seek out the glow,
But sometimes I envy the weeds down below.
They twirl in the wild, while I sit and I pine,
Oh to dance with the daisies—wouldn't that be divine?

So come, little gardener, and give me a chance,
Let's plan for a picnic, invite all to dance.
With a sprinkle of laughter and warm summer air,
I'd throw a parade with my petals laid bare.

So here's my ambition, so clear and so sweet,
To spread joy all 'round with my botanical beat.
I'll rise to the challenge in my pot's little home,
For each day is a journey, and oh, how I roam!

Flora's Silent Song

In the corner, I do stand,
Hoping for a sunny hand.
Water me and say a prayer,
I'll dance a jig, without a care.

Dust mites have a party here,
While I just droop and disappear.
What's that? A broom? Oh dear me!
My leafy party, set me free!

Sometimes I dream of the great outdoors,
But then I hear the open doors.
A bug flies in, and oh what fright!
I hide my leaves, and lose the fight.

Yet here I thrive, with hopes in green,
In this small pot, I reign supreme.
So water me, and let me shine,
This plantly life is truly fine!

The Pulse of Prickly Pear

Oh, prickly friend with spines so bold,
You wear your armor, truth be told.
Yet every hug is a sharp surprise,
I smile while plotting my next disguise.

Sitting in a sunny spot so bright,
I hold my ground, and give a fright.
Passersby may think me bare,
But in my heart, I do not care!

When the cat decides to take a nap,
I make my move, with a little clap.
"Try to tussle? Just bring it on!
I'm tough as nails from dusk till dawn!"

Amidst the chaos of furry friends,
I shine with joy that never ends.
With every poke and playful flare,
I prove my worth, oh prickly pear!

Shadows Under a Sunbeam

Underneath the sunny ray,
I stretch my leaves and play all day.
The light dances, the dust will swirl,
As I sway gently, twirl and whirl.

A wandering fly comes buzzing by,
It tickles me, I can't deny!
I laugh in tiny wiggly moves,
"Oh come on now, let's dance, let's groove!"

The vase nearby gives me a wink,
"Don't be shy, it's time to think!"
But I'm too busy with my game,
In every beam, I shout my name!

As shadows lengthen, I must rest,
In my little pot, I am blessed.
A budding dream in every leaf,
In joyful moments, I find relief.

A Promise in Every Petal

Little blooms with colors bright,
Whisper secrets in the night.
"I'll be fabulous," one said,
"Just wait and see, you'll be well-fed!"

Pollen parties in the breeze,
Bring in bumbles with such ease.
"Don't bother me, I'm on a roll!
These sweet scents are my true goal!"

A petal drops, and I just sigh,
"Must you leave, oh, why oh why?"
Yet laughter ripples through the room,
With every fall, there's still a bloom!

So here I stand, a cheeky sprout,
Adventurous seeds scatter about.
In every petal, joy does dwell,
I promise, life is quite swell!

Parable of a Potted Life

In a pot I sit, a leafy star,
Dreaming of travels, adventures afar.
Breezes tickle my leaves with glee,
Yet here I stay, just sipping tea.

My friends are cacti, sharp and spry,
They laugh at my dreams, they hardly sigh.
"Grow tall!" they shout, "but not too wide!"
As if I could roam, with plant pride!

The sunlight beams, a warm embrace,
But I'll take a trip to outer space.
Oh to be free from this windowsill,
Curtains drawn back, oh what a thrill!

Maybe one day I'll stretch my roots,
Swap my pot for some funky boots.
Until then I'll twirl and sway,
Pretending I'm in a cabaret!

Embrace of Ferny Friends

Oh, my frondy friends, so lush and green,
In our jungle, we're kings and queens.
We gossip in whispers, swap tales under sun,
Life in the shade is always fun!

Each leaf a secret, each stem a prank,
We giggle as the gardener draws a blank.
"Prune us or love us, we shall not care!"
As long as there's light, we'll always share.

The spider plant jumps at every breeze,
While I, the fern, just sway with ease.
Our leafy laughter fills the air,
Who knew being potted could lead to flair?

When the sun sets on our leafy feast,
We throw a party, oh what a beast!
Dance to the rhythm of the watering can,
An indoor rave for the greenest clan!

Hopes Housed Within

Inside my pot, I plot and scheme,
To grow and flourish, oh what a dream!
Though I'm stuck here, day after day,
I'll turn this spot into my cabaret!

The dust bunnies whisper, "Go explore!"
But I'm too busy learning to adore.
Dreaming of vines that stretch and climb,
Count me in for a plant-based rhyme!

I've got ambitions, a leafy flair,
I'll sprout petals with utmost care.
Maybe a bloom, or a cheeky vine,
Please, oh please, give me some sunshine!

When twilight falls; a big reveal,
Life in this pot has its own appeal.
Each new leaf is a sign of glee,
Let them envy my leafy decree!

The Craving for a Drop of Rain

I stare at the sky, it's blue and bright,
But all I want is droplets at night.
A little sprinkle, oh what a tease,
Just a taste of that heavenly breeze!

The sun is hot, it blazes bold,
I'm stuck in this pot, feeling old.
A tiny raindrop could save the day,
Let's start a dance, come out to play!

The birds sing songs, they've got the luck,
While I just wait for a passing truck.
To spray me down, let the puddles form,
A garden frenzy, oh that's the norm!

I'll sway to the rhythm of nature's tune,
With every drip, I'll dance and swoon.
So if you hear of an imminent storm,
Let this potted life take on a new form!

Shades of Desire on a Shelf

In pots so bright, we sit all day,
Counting the sunlight in our own way.
Dreaming of soil, of earth so fine,
Hoping for coffee grounds, a treat divine.

We listen to humans talk and squawk,
While we plot our escape in a quirky clock.
With leaves like banners, waving with glee,
Wishing for freedom—just wait and see!

A splash of water, a sprinkle of care,
Make us feel royal, not just a spare.
But please, no pruning—it's such a fright,
We'll hold our breath till the next moonlight!

Oh, to roam wild in a garden lush,
To greet the critters with a cheerful hush.
For now, dear shelf, we'll stay and pretend,
Our dreams of adventure will never end!

A Breath of Nature's Sigh

Oh, to breathe deep in fresh night air,
Instead of this windowsill, I swear!
The breeze teases tips with a gentle breath,
While I'm stuck here—not living, just death.

The cat prances by, a fluffy invader,
With thoughts of my leaves, I feel much greater.
If only I could offer a little hiss,
And scare off the hen who thinks I'm her kiss!

A dance in the sunlight, I twirl, I sway,
Imagining adventures that lead me away.
Yet here I remain, in my little pot,
Plotting my travel to a big flower spot.

Oh, come my friends, let's gather and scheme,
We'll take back the house and live out our dream!
For today, we'll picture a joyful surprise,
As we stretch our leaves toward the wide, open skies!

The Soft Whisper of Green

In the corner I sit, oh so serene,
Whispering secrets in shades of green.
Polishing leaves, my daily routine,
Hoping to dazzle like a queen in a scene.

The dog wags its tail, thinking I'm great,
While I dream of objects far more ornate.
A garden of colors, of bold and cool dreams,
But I'm stuck in a pot, or so it seems.

With every drop of rain, I feel so alive,
Imagining fields where I truly can thrive.
Beware of the broom that sweeps through our space,
For when it arrives, I might just lose face!

Oh, to dance with daisies, to sway with the breeze,
Instead, I'm confined to this seat with much ease.
A tale of a plant with stories untold,
Waiting for adventures, bold and uncontrolled!

Secrets of the Sunlit Corner

In the sunlit nook where the shadows play,
I plot my escape like a green cabaret.
With laughter we twinkle, leaves in array,
Yearning for sunlight at the end of the day.

"Oh, brush me lightly," I might call out,
"To dance in the sunlight, let's twist and shout!"
The dust bunnies giggle, the books stand still,
While we bloom in silence with whimsical will.

If I had a wish, oh, what would it be?
To jump from this shelf and run wild and free!
To mingle with flowers, share roots and some tales,
Not worry 'bout petals or withering scales.

But here I shall stay, with my pot and my dirt,
Waiting for moments that make my heart flirt.
In each little breeze, in each glimmering ray,
There's magic in waiting, come what may!

Whimsy Amongst Sills

In the corner sunbeam, I stretch so high,
Waiting for a breeze to make me sigh.
Poke me gently, give me a dance,
I'll twirl my leaves, come join the prance!

Oh, look at me, a green little star,
Dreaming of vacations, just wander far.
A pot so tiny, my roots are cramped,
I might just burst, oh, how I've champed!

The cat jumps by, with a swat and a grin,
I'm not a toy, won't wear a chin!
But here I am, all soft and spry,
Come take a selfie, oh me, oh my!

When night falls down, I close my eyes,
Counting the bugs that flit and fly.
One day I'll grow, plant dreams in sight,
For now, I'll just drink in the light!

Soliloquy of Succulents

Oh, to be a cactus, bold and brash,
With needles like armor, in a prickly clash.
I'd hold my ground, no need to flee,
And laugh at the drought, come sip some tea!

A jade's my neighbor, shiny and bright,
Sipping on sunshine both day and night.
While I hoard water in thick, plump skin,
The gardener wonders where I begin!

If only I could dance, twist, and twirl,
With spiky confetti, I'd give it a whirl.
Oh, the zany tales we could tell,
Of dance-offs at dusk, or waltzing so well!

But here I sit, in a pot of clay,
Peering out the window, longing for play.
So raise your glass to us greens on display,
For we just wish for a fun-filled day!

Tales Traced in Chloroplasts

Once I saw a sunflower, tall and proud,
Waving at the clouds, talking loud.
I tried to join in, but fell quite shy,
Imagining wild tales of the sky!

With 'chlorophyll quips,' I'd share my lore,
While my leafy friends would beg for more.
But can you hear me? Oh, what a sight,
As I spill my secrets in the warm sunlight!

The fern was snoozing, lost in a dream,
While I crafted verse with a leafy gleam.
"Let's start a club, just for us greens!
We'll plot all our escapes, and share the scenes!"

But alas, the window is sealed up tight,
A house full of chores, where's the delight?
Tiny visions of adventures rise high,
Hoping one day to dance in the sky!

A Craving for Cracks of Light

In a room full of shadows, I stretch for the sun,
Peeking through curtains, oh, let it come!
Each sliver of gold, a treasure so rare,
I twiddle my leaves, as if to declare!

Mom's watering can brings giggles galore,
As I play hide and seek on the floor.
"Just a drop here," she says with a grin,
While I wink back, ready to spin!

Oh how I envy those bright, sunny spots,
While I sip on the drips from the kitchen pots.
I dream of a sky, so ocean-like blue,
And daydream of sunbeams, so soft and so new!

Maybe one day, I'll burst out with glee,
Exploring the world, just a wild green spree.
For now, I'll chuckle, in my little plight,
Craving the joy of those cracks of light!

Quiet Resilience in Clay

In a pot that's snug and round,
I dream of sunbeams all around.
Inside these walls, I sway and wiggle,
Yet my roots, they dance, oh so giggle.

With every droplet, I take a sip,
A tiny leaf does a happy flip.
I adorn this corner, bright and green,
But who knew I could have such a scene?

When dust gets thick, I huff and puff,
With soil and sunlight, I'm pretty tough.
If only I could stretch my leaves,
To poke at folks, oh how I'd tease!

So here I stand, in my pot of clay,
Wishing for laughter, come what may!
Life's a show, and I play my part,
With roots so deep and a crafty heart.

The Solace of Tiny Buds

Beneath the light, I take my seat,
Tiny buds, oh what a treat!
They bulge and bulge, so eager to grow,
While I'm just here, putting on a show.

My neighbor's cactus is prickly and mean,
I pretend I'm regal, the queen of green.
In my little patch, I spin tiny tales,
Of daring escapes from the house cat's gales.

Each day, I stretch with flair and grace,
Imagining life beyond this space.
With each new leaf, I giggle and sing,
"Look at me! I'm the plant, the thing!"

So here's to buds and green delight,
With quirky roots that dance in light.
A garden party, just waiting to bloom,
In my plastic pot with so much room!

Hope Hiding in High Shelves

Perched high above in a dusty nook,
I plot my escape with a greenish look.
The view is grand, I can see it all,
While down below, the dust bunnies crawl.

My siblings below just sigh and sway,
But I'm up here, it's a glorious day!
I can see the snacks, the fun, and cheer,
While they wait for water, I sip on air.

"Oh, fetch me down!" they start to whine,
But I quite like it, this sunshine shrine.
With every glance, I twirl and preen,
While they lament their life unseen.

I count the days till I'm down and free,
To frolic in soil, to play, you see.
But for now, I enjoy my height,
Dreaming of gardens, frolicking at night!

Composed in Nature's Chorus

In the window's light, I sway with glee,
An elegant dance, just my leaves and me.
The birds outside give quite the show,
While I'm here practicing my flow.

Each little breeze makes me bob and twist,
A green little diva, too fun to resist.
"Watch me!" I laugh, twirling with flair,
As neighbor's dog stares with a blank glare.

With sunlit hugs, I simply can't fail,
While critters below wag their tiny tails.
Nature's choir plays a tune just right,
As I serenade the day into night.

So here's my song, simple and true,
A laugh, a chuckle, a leaf or two.
With roots in the soil and dreams above,
I dance through my days, sharing the love.

Yearning for the Sunshine

Oh, to stretch my leaves out wide,
And bask in playful rays of pride.
Instead I'm stuck in this old pot,
Just dreaming of the warmth I've sought.

I see the window, it's so bright,
While I'm here in the shade all night.
A sunbeam's touch, what a delight,
But here I wait, avoiding fright.

Let's trade this gloom for some bright cheer,
I promise not to whine or sneer.
Just one good sip from the golden beam,
And I'll glow bright—oh, what a dream!

So please, dear friend, crack wide that shade,
Let sunlight sparkle, let it invade.
A dance of joy, I'll do it well,
If only you'd give me that spell!

The Quiet Life of Leaves

In the corner, quietly I sit,
With dust bunnies that refuse to quit.
I dream of breezes, oh so grand,
But here I am, just waiting, bland.

The neighbor's fern is having fun,
While I'm stuck here, not on the run.
He's swaying lightly, feeling spry,
And I just watch while I sigh and sigh.

If only I could join the breeze,
I'd leap and swirl with effortless ease.
But here I lounge, a sleepy soul,
Wishing for a more lively role.

The moments pass, the sunlight fades,
Yet still I wait beneath the shades.
With every hour, I hope and pine,
For a little shake, a sign divine!

Cradled in Humidity

Oh, let me soak in moisture deep,
Where I can sprout and happily leap.
Sweaty, sticky, what a treat,
The air wraps 'round me, oh so sweet!

I dream of rain dancing on leaves,
Where every droplet gently weaves.
But here I sit, all dry and stark,
Wishing for mist, not just the dark.

So sprinkle me with all you've got,
I promise I won't turn to rot.
Just a little humidity, please,
And I'll thrive like a breeze through trees!

Come on, let's make this fun and bright,
Be my gardener, bring delight.
A splash, a spray; oh, what a thrill,
I'll grow so tall, if you just will!

The Dance of Dust Motions

In the sunbeam, dust goes twirling,
Round and round, it's freely whirling.
While here I stand, all calm and still,
I wish to join, if just for the thrill.

Watch those particles, how they play,
I long to dance, just for a day.
But all I've got are roots below,
And in my pot, I can't quite flow.

If only I could take a chance,
To leap and twirl in a silly dance.
Instead I watch from this dusty throne,
While dust bunnies claim my zone alone.

So let me sway, let me feel the breeze,
A little jig—to say just please!
In my quiet world, I'd surely shine,
If only you'd help me cross that line!

The Yearn of Verdant Adventure

In a pot with great delight,
I dream of climbing up to height.
To bask beneath the golden sun,
Oh, the fun has just begun!

With a sprout on my head, I scheme,
To live my jungle fantasy dream.
Imagining vines in thick green wraps,
And maybe a few friendly naps!

A squirrel swings by, says hello,
'You'd thrive if you just let it grow!'
Yet here I sit, soil-bound and meek,
Plotting escapes with a peek.

I long to dance in a wild breeze,
Not just swaying 'neath the trees.
Oh, to explore with roots anew,
But here I water, feeling blue!

Emotions in Every Stem

My leaves are green and full of zest,
Yet my feelings often rest.
I wish to twirl in floral cheer,
But it's quiet here—oh dear!

The neighbor plant just had a bloom,
My envy causes me some gloom.
Yet I talk to the bugs and bees,
Sharing secrets through the leaves.

Every droplet brings a grin,
But who will come and spin with me?
The sun is bright, the clouds are few,
I'll stretch my leaves for something new!

Oh, to feel those happy vibes,
To roll with winds, join nature's jibes.
But I keep my roots deep and true,
As I daydream of sky so blue!

A Stillness in Growth

In silence I stretch, no rush at all,
Watching the raindrops start to fall.
Day by day, I inch my way,
Imagining I could someday sway!

I try to chat with folks who pass,
But they just stare, and I feel crass.
I whisper jokes to the tiny bugs,
While pondering the art of shrugs.

When the cats prance by, I joke,
'At least my pot isn't a yoke!'
Their fur flies loose, my leaves stay still,
Who knew this life could bring such thrill?

So give me time, let growth unfold,
As I bask in sunlight, bright and bold.
Though stationary and very grand,
In this pot, I plant my stand!

The Connection of Chlorophyll

Oh green friend, you've got the flair,
Chlorophyll magic fills the air.
Let's blend our thoughts, join leafy fun,
Sharing glances in the morning sun!

When shadows linger, I sing so sweet,
To entertain the roots beneath my feet.
We cheer for sunshine, giggle with rains,
Life's better shared from our plant domains.

So here we grow, side by side,
In this lively pot, there's no need to hide.
We'll set the vibe, all plants unite,
Offering bursts of color, pure delight!

With every breath, we share our glee,
Living legends of the greenery.
In every rustle, hear the sound,
Of friendship forged in soil profound!

Flourish and Fade

In a corner, I stand tall,
Chasing sunlight, not much at all.
My leaves, they twist and then they bend,
Whispering secrets, my only friends.

Water me twice, it's all I ask,
Don't put me anywhere near that flask.
If I could dance, I'd shimmy and shake,
But rooted here, it's all a fake.

Dust me off; I've got a plan,
To grow a flower, yes I can!
But then the cats come tumbling by,
And I just sigh, oh me, oh my.

As seasons change, I watch in glee,
My little pot, it brings me tea.
Baffle me not with fancy talk,
Just give me sun and let me rock!

Serenity in a Shouldered Pot

In a pot that's far too tight,
I dream of being bold and bright.
But humans think I like to hide,
As they parade me, pot and pride.

I've grown a leaf, but just one pair,
While others boast a jungle flair.
If only I could stretch out wide,
Perhaps they'd take me on a ride.

Serenity, oh what a tease,
To sip on water, not the tease.
Prune my edges, give me cheer,
As I roll my leaves to wave near.

Life's a party, can't you see?
I'm just a plant; let me be free.
No high society, no grand show,
Just time to grow and let it flow!

The Illumination of Life

In gentle light, I dream and glow,
Pick me up, and let's take it slow.
Photosynthesis is my game,
But please don't scold me if I'm tame.

The sun, it shines, my golden friend,
Together, let our bright times blend.
I stretch my leaves, oh, what delight,
Just getting warmed up feels so right.

But sprinkle me with droplets small,
Oh human, don't you let it fall!
Give me a show of watering can,
And I shall dance like no one's plan.

Illumination? My daily goal,
With raindrops glistening, that's my role.
So here I stand, a leafy sight,
Oh, life's so funny when it's bright!

Petals Pondering Paths

Petals ponder paths unknown,
Where to wander, they've not grown.
Shall I climb? Or maybe slide?
Or just lounge here, a plant-bum wide?

A world outside, so vast and grand,
But I'm stuck in this little land.
Occasionally, I hear them chat,
They say, 'Look at that silly plant!'

I long for wind to toss me near,
To feel the grass and taste the beer.
But alas, I stay in this spot,
With budding dreams, I laugh a lot.

So here I dwell, with heart so spry,
As sunny days just zoom on by.
Petals dreaming, leaves in flight,
Oh, what a mess, this plant's delight!

A Desire for the Open Sky

Oh, to stretch my leaves so wide,
Not just to grow, but to glide.
When pots become a tiny cage,
I dream of flying like a sage.

Birds up high, they laugh and sing,
While I just sway and feel the sting.
A breeze would tickle, light and free,
Instead, I dance to a stuck routine.

If only clouds would whisper low,
I'd trade my soil for skies to tow.
What joy to feel that sunlit air,
A plant's life trapped, it's just not fair.

But here I sit, all green and meek,
While squirrels mug me with their cheek.
Yet still I bloom, my petals bright,
Hoping for freedom, oh what a sight!

Flora's Gentle Refrain

I sigh each morn, a leafy tune,
Peeking out beneath the moon.
Stuck in the window, I beg for more,
If only I could strut outdoors!

My neighbor's cat goes sprawled in sun,
While I just sit—oh, isn't that fun?
To bathe in rays without a wall,
Instead, I'm shouting, "Let me call!"

A gentle breeze, a flirt or two,
Who knew that nature's love could brew?
But here I dangle on this string,
Just a hint of outdoor fling.

So I might sway and gently croon,
But in my heart, I'm over the moon.
Just one adventure, a dash of cheer,
To leap from pot—let's make it clear!

An Unspoken Dialogue with the Sun

Each dawn I chat with glowing rays,
As I sit here for countless days.
"My friend," I whisper, "let's take a spin,
What's life like, where your dances begin?"

But trapped in this cozy nook,
I plot my routes, I dream, I look.
While you rise high, amidst the flair,
I'm here, just pondering stale air.

Sunshine's laughter rhymes so sweet,
Yet my little roots know no defeat.
I stretch and shimmy, I wave my arms,
But potted life has its own charms!

Oh to be wild, a sprawling vine,
But here I am, sipping water fine.
Still, a secret joy blooms deep inside,
In my pot, I've learned to abide.

Craving the Caress of Wind

Dear gentle gust, how I miss your kiss,
In this room, it's a plant's big abyss.
I hear the whispers through the glass,
Reminding me of freedom's class.

Stuck with soil, I bob and nod,
Yet all I daydream, is to trod.
A dance with leaves that whirl and spin,
An outdoor life, where do I begin?

Oh, how the air could tease my stem,
While I'm stashed in this little gem.
Nature's arms would wrap me tight,
But for now, it's just my cozy plight.

With every shake, I summon cheer,
Yet yearn for winds that gust and steer.
So here I sit, a patient sprout,
Ready to break free, without a doubt!

Vows of the Verdant

To stay green forever, I pledge with glee,
No wilting for me, I'm quite plant-astic!
I'll cheer up the room, just wait and see,
With my leafy dance, most enthusiastic!

I promise to sway, at the light's first beam,
A happy little jig in my earthen dome.
Oh how I long for that sunlit dream,
To bask and to bloom, in my cozy home!

No spider mites here, I'll shout with pride,
Keep those pests away, or I'll make a ruckus!
With my photosynthesis as my guide,
I'll spin around and put on a circus!

So here's to my friends, who often forget,
To water my roots or give me a chat.
As long as you love me, there's no regret,
I'll thrive in your company, especially where it's at!

In Search of the Perfect Ray

Oh, light of my life, how I crave your glow,
Just not too much heat, that's a plant's woe.
I've scouted the windows, from north to south,
Seeking that sweet spot, I'm on the prowl!

The sunbeam's dance is quite a sight to see,
But I won't fight off a moth or a bee.
Bright mornings buzz with promises fair,
And I'll stretch out my leaves, not a single care.

I've tried the bathroom, but it feels like a trap,
The steam is so loud, I can't take a nap!
The living room's comfy but lacks a flair,
I'll continue my quest, till I find that perfect air.

Oh, glorious light, my leafy delight,
When you find your home, it will feel so right.
For now, I'll just sit and hope for the best,
In a pot full of dreams, I'll continue my quest!

The Embrace of Potting Soil

Oh, sweet potting soil, you're the best of friends,
In your earthy embrace, all my troubles end.
With a sprinkle of water, I'll flourish anew,
Together we'll rise, just me and you!

Your grains are so cozy, I nestle with care,
A cushion for roots, a soft, nurturing layer.
I might take a trip to the bottom, I fear,
But your warm, cuddly hugs always bring me cheer.

Sometimes a worm wanders, thinking it's grand,
But I'll show them who's boss, they must understand!
With a twist and a turn, I'll give 'em a show,
In this potting party, I'm the star, don't you know?

So let's raise a toast, with my leafy green arm,
To the soil beneath me, my favorite charm.
In this earthly dance, I'll spin and delight,
Underneath the moon, through many a night!

Echoes of Growth

In the corner I stand, a tribute to time,
Echoes of growth in the morning's prime.
With every new leaf, I shout and sing,
"Look at me! I'm a verdant king!"

The neighbors all stare as I reach for the sky,
With my abundant greens, I can't be shy.
"Is that a fern?" they whisper in awe,
"Nope, just me being fabulous, here's my flaw!"

I've watched my pals come and maybe they fade,
But I'm here thriving, a leafy crusade.
Every inch I gain is a tale to tell,
In the jungle of home, I'm ringing my bell!

So tiptoe on by, lest you tread on my dreams,
For in this new pot, I'm bursting at seams.
With laughter and roots, I'll happily grow,
The echoes of growth are the best kind of show!

The Journey of a Leaf

A little leaf set off one day,
Waving goodbye to the pot's bouquet.
"I want to see the world so wide,
And not just sit here, all dignified!"

It tumbled down and rolled so free,
"Where will I go?" it sang with glee.
Past sneaky cats and muddy shoes,
"Oh, plants can roam! Who knew? Who knew?"

Found a ladybug, they danced a jig,
He said, "Oh, Leaf, you're quite the twig!"
They laughed and shared stories of the sun,
"Come back, dear pot, you're missing the fun!"

But soon the wind began to blow,
And Leaf got nervous, felt all aglow.
"I think it's time to head back home,
This journey's great, but oh, I miss my loam!"

Petals in the Moonlight

At midnight's hour, the petals dance,
In silver light, they take their chance.
"Look at me, I'm quite the sight!"
Said Daisy to Rose, in pure delight.

"If I can sway, so must you!"
"Let's show the stars what we can do!"
They spun and twirled, oh what a show,
Two pretty flowers stealing the glow.

A bumblebee came buzzing by,
"What's this racket?" he let out a sigh.
"Can't a bee nap in peace tonight?"
"Don't mind us! We're high on delight!"

Then came a gust that stole their grace,
Petals flying all over the place!
"Oh dear, catch me if you can!"
Squealed the flowers, in roguish plan.

Serenity in a Terracotta Pot

In a sunny nook, sits a pot so round,
"It's my fortress here on solid ground!"
Said the fern with a calming sway,
"Life's pretty chill, come what may!"

But then entered a feisty sprout,
"Come on, Fern, let's go about!"
"Adventure awaits beyond this fence!"
"I'm not so sure, but I'll take a chance!"

The pot wobbled, it felt alive,
"Hold on, let's see how we can thrive!"
With laughter shared, off they did roam,
Finding wild weeds that felt like home.

Later on, they sat and sighed,
"What fun we had, I was terrified!"
But serenity still called the shot,
"Next time, dear friend, let's not get caught!"

Hopes Climbing the Trellis

Trellis tall, oh what a sight!
With dreams of heights, a plant took flight.
"I'll climb so high, just wait and see,"
Cried the vine with utmost glee.

As it wriggled up, it fancied fame,
"I'll be in the news! They'll know my name!"
Got tangled up, what a twist!
"Oh dear me, I just can't resist!"

A bird passed by and chuckled loud,
"Look at you, lost in a leafy cloud!"
"Oh hush! I'm reaching for the sky,
One day, I swear, I'll give it a try!"

Then came a breeze, oh what a glee,
"With every gust, I'm wild and free!"
But forgot the pot still held it tight,
"My lovely home, you're my guiding light!"

Yearning for the Light

Oh, I stretch my leaves so high,
Hoping warmth will pass me by.
Is it too much to implore,
Just a little sun, please more?

My friends are all so lush and bright,
While I sit in this gloomy sight.
Photosynthesis, oh what a tease,
Give me rays, I'm begging, please!

The window's closed, a cruel fate,
I'm stuck with shadows while others elate.
With every inch of dusty pane,
I whisper, brighten up this lane!

One day I'll bask, my chance will come,
Till then I dance, though oh so glum.
Just a flicker, oh glorious spark,
I'll serenade the sun till dark!

A Leaf's Soliloquy

I'm just a leaf, not much to see,
But oh, the dreams inside of me.
With every droplet, every spray,
I ponder life's strange little play.

Photosynthesis? Sounds divine!
But this pot? It feels like a shrine.
I'm crammed in here, not quite a clown,
But I could shine if freed from brown!

I'll sway and shimmy, that's my plan,
If only movement didn't ban.
So here I am, just wiggling slow,
In hopes that sunlight starts the show.

When the sunshine spills, I'll show my flair,
And grow a mane of leafy hair.
For now, I'll sigh and dream of glee,
A leaf's soliloquy, just me and me!

The Dance of Dust and Sun

In morning sun, I twirl with dust,
Their particles dance; oh, it's a must.
With fronds up high, I tap my toes,
To rhythms only the sunlight knows.

The dust bunnies cheer, they know my plight,
In corners I yearn for a sliver of light.
A fan, a breeze, a wild little whirl,
I'm the belle of the room, give me a twirl!

Each beam that beams feels so sublime,
As I sway and groove, losing track of time.
Though shadows loom, I won't be undone,
I'm grooving 'til night, 'til setting sun!

So pass me a beam, bright and bold,
Together we'll dance, my story told.
With dust as my partner, and cheer in my heart,
Let's sway through the day, a merry art!

Cradled in Clay

Oh, this clay pot is snug and tight,
Cozy as a bug on a chilly night.
Yet sometimes I dream of meadow green,
Beyond the window, a blissful scene.

Roots all tangled, in a twisty race,
Wishing to stretch, oh, what a place!
But here I sit, with soil so dank,
Just waiting for my leafy prank.

Water me now or I'll pout all day,
I've got some charm—don't walk away!
With a sip or two, I start to glow,
In this muddy home, let's steal the show!

Cradled in clay, I'll wear a grin,
As sunshine trickles, my dance begins.
Oh, pot of mine, take heed, I say,
With just a little love, I'll find my way!

The Longing of a Fickle Fern

In a pot that's far too tight,
I yearn for freedom, oh what a sight!
If only I could dance and sway,
I'd show the world I'm here to play.

But then the cat comes prowling near,
With stealthy steps, oh dear, oh dear!
I curl up small, don't make a fuss,
Yet dream of jungles, just me and us.

Underneath the sunny rays,
I plot my schemes on lazy days.
Should I grab that sunbeam wide?
Or just bask here with feline pride?

Oh, to chat with a cactus friend,
Discussing luck and the curves we bend.
Yet here I sit, what a silly plight,
Wishing for adventures in the night.

Roots Sweeping Through Time

My roots are tangled, oh what a tale,
Of travels within and a wondrous trail.
As I sip the water, I daydream loud,
About the places where I could crowd.

To sip on the dew from the mountain top,
Or take a dip near the vibrant shop.
But alas, I'm stuck in this living room,
Just sneaking glances, oh how I bloom!

With an ear to the ground, I hear them speak,
Stories of ferns who went to seek.
A jaunt through the soil, a romp through the grass,
While I sit here in a vase made of glass.

I wish for a breeze, a whirl and a twirl,
Not just the sound of that purring girl.
Yet I must admit, this sun is quite nice,
But freedom is surely worth any price!

Dreams Crafted in Green

In the corner, I stretch and sigh,
Watching the world as it flits by.
If I could wiggle, oh what a scene,
I'd turn my pot into a machine!

A ride to the cafe, sipping my tea,
With crispy carrots and smoothie for me.
But here I am, with muck in my roots,
Wishing for more than just wilted shoots.

I've heard of the plants that fly high above,
With vines intertwined, full of love.
And while I sway to the music of air,
My dreams take flight, without a care.

For in my heart, I'm a wild flower,
Plotting my journey in perfect hour.
So here's to the chaos of sweet little things,
As I pretend to have my own wings!

The Lullaby of Leaves

As night drops its curtain, I feel a shift,
Wishing on stars for a magical lift.
If only the breeze could carry me far,
I'd dance with the moon, oh what a bizarre!

Yet here I am, clinging to my pot,
Dreaming of breezes in my little spot.
With whispers of tales from the great outdoors,
I chuckle softly at my leafy chores.

My friends, the daisies, tell me to chill,
They sway and giggle, they've got such skill.
But how do I wear a flower crown?
Stuck in this pot, on the brink of a frown!

Oh, to tickle the clouds with a daring leap,
Instead of napping in this planty heap.
But tomorrow, my dreams will take flight anew,
With laughter and sunlight, I'm never blue!

www.ingramcontent.com/pod-product-compliance
Lightning Source LLC
Chambersburg PA
CBHW070311120526
44590CB00017B/2625